This library edition published in 2011 by Walter Foster Publishing, Inc.
Walter Foster Library
Distributed by Black Rabbit Books.
P.O. Box 3263 Mankato, Minnesota 56002

Printed in China by CT PRINTING, Shenzhen.

First Library Edition

Library of Congress Cataloging-in-Publication Data

McCafferty, Catherine.
  Learn to draw princesses / written by Catherine McCafferty. -- 1st library ed.
    p. cm.
  At head of title: Disney princess
  ISBN 978-1-936309-23-8 (hardcover)
  1. Princesses in art--Juvenile literature. 2. Drawing--Technique--Juvenile
literature. I. Title. II. Title: Princesses. III. Title: Disney princess.
  NC825.P75M39 2011
  743.4'4--dc22

                                                2010004208

022010
0P1816

9 8 7 6 5 4 3 2 1

How to Draw PRINCESSES

Disney Princess

Disney princesses can be found in a fairy-tale castle, an enchanted wood, a French countryside, a desert kingdom—even under the sea! Although their stories may be similar—overcoming problems to reach "happily ever after"—each princess brings something special to her tale. Over the years, that "something special" has changed, but the beauty and love that shine in each princess have always remained the same.

Written by
Catherine McCafferty

Getting Started

sharpener

graphite pencil
and paper

Tools and Materials

You'll want to gather a few simple supplies to create your own Disney princesses world. Try starting with a graphite pencil, so you can easily erase any mistakes (don't forget to grab an eraser too!). Then you can add color with markers, crayons, colored pencils, watercolor, or acrylic paint. It's up to you!

eraser

felt-tip
markers

paintbrush
and paints

2

How to Use This Book

You can draw any princess by following the simple steps in this book. You'll be amazed at how fun and easy drawing can be!

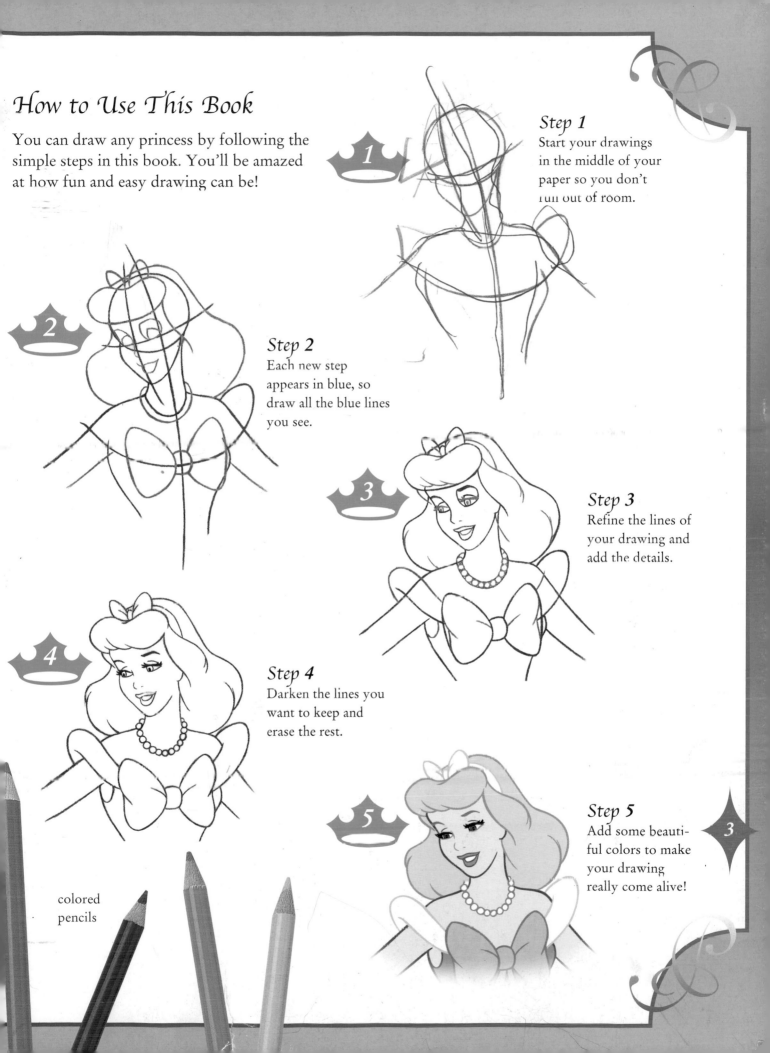

Step 1
Start your drawings in the middle of your paper so you don't run out of room.

Step 2
Each new step appears in blue, so draw all the blue lines you see.

Step 3
Refine the lines of your drawing and add the details.

Step 4
Darken the lines you want to keep and erase the rest.

colored pencils

Step 5
Add some beautiful colors to make your drawing really come alive!

3

Snow White

Snow White is a beautiful young princess who is badly mistreated by her wicked stepmother, the Queen. When creating Snow White, Walt Disney decided to make his first feature princess look more like a pretty "girl next door" than like a glamorous princess. Snow White does have rose-red lips, ebony hair, and skin as white as snow that win her the title of "fairest one of all." But her rounded face and figure also show her youth and innocence.

NO! bridge of Snow White's nose not seen unless in profile (side view)

Snow White's hair is drawn with soft curves

eyelashes curl out from her eyelids

top lip is thinner than bottom lip

lips are soft and not too full

Snow White's
features follow
these guidelines

Snow White

Even when she's abandoned in the forest, Snow White's kindness shines through and wins her the friendship of all the forest animals—as well as the love and loyalty of all of the Seven Dwarfs. When you draw Snow White, be sure to show the soft, sweeping lines in her dress and the gentle arm movements that emphasize her cheerful, sweet disposition and her joy for life.

Snow White's hands are rounded and soft like this . . .

. . . not sharp and pointed like this

draw the legs as a guide, even though they're covered by skirt

YES! skirt is wider than hips

NO! skirt is too close to hips

feet are small and delicate

4

3

5

Snow White is about 6 heads tall

lines are graceful, with no sharp angles

NO! *not angular*

figure is rounded

NO! *not too curvy*

Cinderella

Cinderella's story seems much like Snow White's at first: Cinderella is treated badly by her stepfamily, but she overcomes all to win the love of a prince. She is also as pretty as can be, whether she appears as a simple house maiden with her hair pulled back or as a glamorous ball guest with her hair swept up. Still, Cinderella is a very different kind of princess than Snow White is. Whereas Snow White wishes and waits for her love to appear, Cinderella wills her dreams to come true, and she goes to find her Prince Charming at the ball.

1

2

YES! Cinderella's waist is full but not too plump

NO! waist is not so thin

 Cinderella has almond-shaped eyes

YES! eyelids have slight S-curve

 NO! not droopy— avoid sad eyes

YES! just slight
suggestion of nose

NO! nose is not a
full shape

YES! head-
band curves
only a little

headband is
straighter on top
than on side

NO! too round

9

Cinderella

Cinderella's beauty and graceful movements are evident as she runs down the stairs in her simple, homemade gown, but they are even more obvious at the ball. When she first arrives in her gorgeous dress (thanks to her Fairy Godmother), she immediately attracts everyone's attention, including Prince Charming's. When you draw her sweeping gown with billowing curves, show just a bit of the elegant lace underneath.

10

1

Cinderella's fingers are long and slender

YES! angles are soft and smooth

NO! angles are not sharp

2

Cinderella is about 6-1/2 heads tall

11

Sleeping Beauty

Though 16-year-old Princess Aurora has been gifted with beauty, she looks very different from both Snow White and Cinderella. She appears older—more like a woman than like a young girl. Princess Aurora spends the early years of her life in the forest as the "peasant" Briar Rose, where she wears a simple dress and holds back her wavy, waist-length hair with a headband. This is how she looks when she first meets Prince Phillip.

1

YES! Sleeping Beauty's hair extends behind head at an angle

NO! not straight down the back of head

2

eyes tilt up slightly

YES! eyes end in pointed corners and have one thick eyelash

NO! not round— don't draw individual lashes

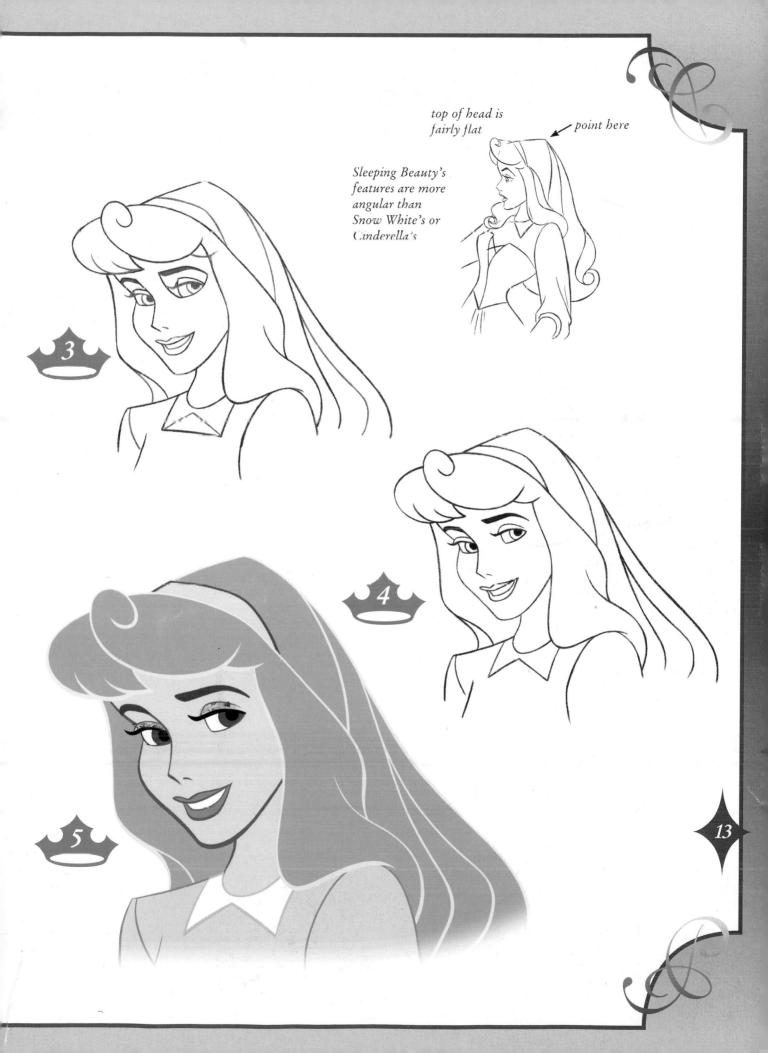

top of head is
fairly flat

← *point here*

*Sleeping Beauty's
features are more
angular than
Snow White's or
Cinderella's*

13

Sleeping Beauty

When Aurora is awakened from her sleep by a kiss from Prince Phillip, she is saved from the curse placed upon her at birth—and she gets to marry her true love! Now when she dances with her prince in the palace, her simple dress is exchanged for a lovely gown, and a beautiful tiara replaces her plain headband. Use long, slightly curved lines for her skirt to show how regal this princess has become.

Sleeping Beauty's hair curls like this at the back

when she dances, hair swings out like this

14

3

4

5

Sleeping Beauty
is about 6-1/2
heads tall

waist is
very slim

large bangs
on left

big curl
on right

YES! curls
are closed,
like this

NO! not
open curls

15

Ariel

In many ways, *The Little Mermaid's* Ariel starts out as a very different character from Snow White, Cinderella, or Aurora. She is a confident, headstrong, and passionate teenager who knows exactly what she wants—and will do anything to get it. In fact, she is a princess among princesses, with no fewer than six royal sisters! Ariel lives with her sisters and her father, King Triton, under the sea in Atlantica. And her wavy red hair—a new hair color for a Disney princess—flows with the currents in her underwater kingdom.

16

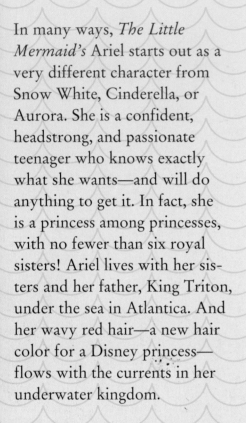

YES! Ariel's bangs pouf out over her forehead

NO! hair doesn't cover face

YES! Ariel's eyes are wedge-shaped

NO! not triangular . . .

. . . nor round

YES! lips are smooth curves

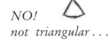

NO! there's no "dimple" on top lip

hair billows out, especially underwater

each eyebrow is
one thin line

← YES! thin
eyebrows

NO! not thick

YES! oval nose is
angled like this

NO! not hori-
zontal like this

17

Ariel

Ariel probably changes the most of any of the princesses—physically, at least. To get her prince, she trades her voice for legs and feet so she can live on the land. But even without speaking, she's able to win the heart of Prince Eric. Try drawing her as we first meet her, wearing her seashell mermaid outfit and swimming freely under the sea.

Ariel's body curves more behind . . .

. . . and curves less in front

1

Ariel is about 6-1/2 heads tall from the top of her hair to the tip of her fins

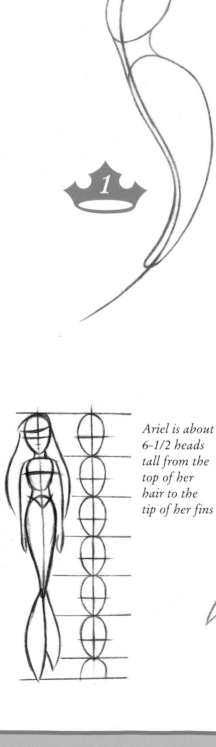

2

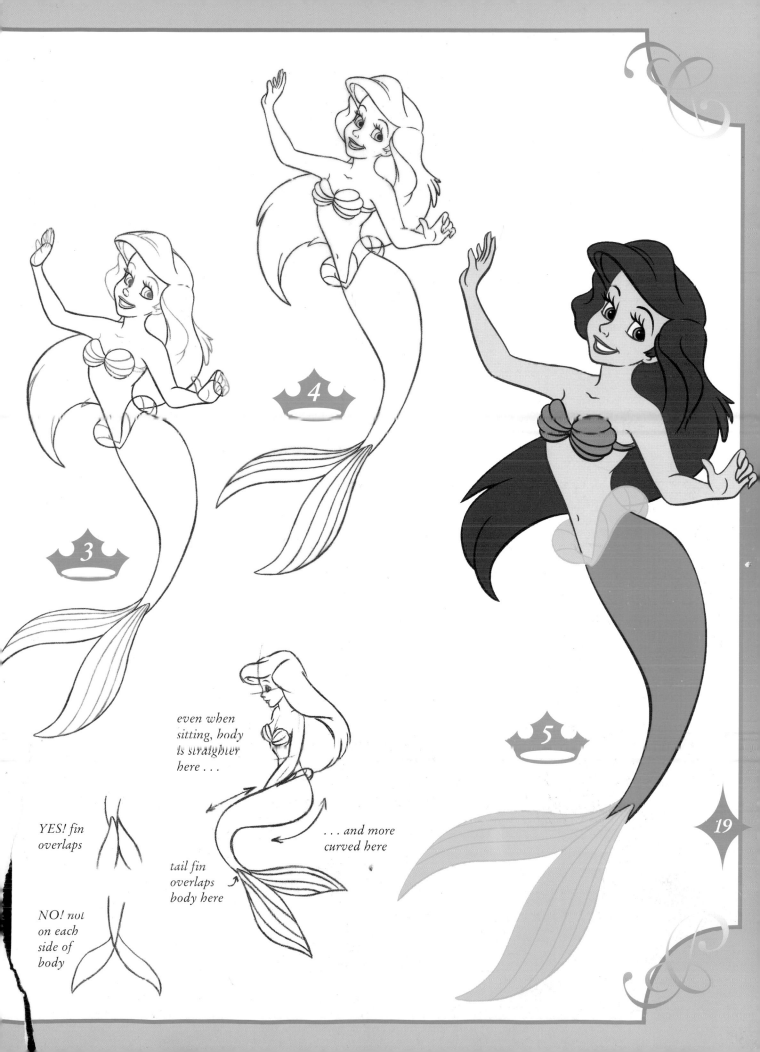

4

3

even when
sitting, body
is straighter
here . . .

. . . and more
curved here

tail fin
overlaps
body here

YES! fin
overlaps

NO! not
on each
side of
body

5

19

Belle

Beauty and the Beast's Belle may like to read and daydream about princes and princesses, but she doesn't live the life of royalty. And she certainly isn't looking for a prince—especially if the closest thing to a "prince" in her town is the conceited Gaston! Down-to-earth Belle keeps her brown hair pulled back in a simple ponytail as she leads a "normal life" in her small, provincial town. Her large, almond-shaped eyes capture the sense of wonder and excitement she feels about new ideas and new places.

1

2

YES! Belle's have s angles

angle

angle

NO! not smooth oval

Belle has simple features

nose is fairly long with defined bridge

thin upper lip

YES! upper lip is thinner than lower lip

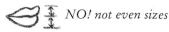 NO! not even sizes

YES! eyebrows are smooth and thin

NO! not thick or angular

Belle's facial features follow these guidelines

1

2/3

1/3

0

hair bow extends beyond chin line

4

3

when eyes close, angle of eyes is less dramatic

5

21

Belle

Belle's prince is horrifying at first—a handsome man trapped in the body of a hideous-looking beast. But Belle soon warms up to his gentle nature, and when she prepares to join the Beast for dinner, she dresses in a beautiful ball gown and wears a hair style befitting a princess. Draw Belle in her elegant, yellow gown, ready to waltz with the Beast in the grand ballroom.

when worn down, Belle's hair is drawn with simple shapes that wrap around her head

YES! hair curves around head

NO! no straight line across head

in ponytail, hair is pulled close to head

*Belle is about
6-1/2 heads tall*

Jasmine

Like Aurora, *Aladdin's* Jasmine is about to have her fateful 16th birthday at the beginning of her story. But while Aurora's fairy "aunts" kept hopeful princes away, Jasmine's father hopes that his daughter will marry one of the many princes who come to see her. But Jasmine has other ideas. She would rather marry for love—and she chooses the handsome, young street thief, Aladdin. Jasmine's dramatic features emphasize her exotic beauty, making her unique among the Disney princesses.

Jasmine has almond-shaped eyes

top of eye has flatter curve

bottom of eye has rounder curve

Jasmine's eyes have gentle slant, like cat's eyes

YES! eyes follow bottom of guide-line circle

NO! not straight across face

eyes are about 1 eye-width apart

thick eyebrows

hair overlaps eyebrows

full bottom lip

3

4

5

YES! back of hair comes out to soft point

NO! not round; not so small

Jasmine

Jasmine's outfit gives her the freedom and flexibility to move quickly—whether she is running away from Aladdin (posing as Prince Ali) or from the evil Jafar. But she looks just as graceful as the other princesses do in their fancy ball gowns, and every bit a princess. Be sure to draw the sparkling jewel in her headband and the curled toes of her delicate slippers.

Jasmine's arms are slender and graceful

elbows fall at waist line

1

2

YES! head-band curves around head like this

NO! not straight like this

Jasmine is just a little more than 5 heads tall

YES! Tinker Bell's eyes are slightly tilted but still have rounded shape

NO! not narrow ovals; no pointed corners

Tinker Bell is both a loyal friend and an overprotective fairy when it comes to Peter Pan. And she has an impish presence all her own. Wherever she goes, a trail of pixie dust follows, and her voice sounds like the tinkling of tiny bells. Tinker Bell's pixie look is carried through in her hair style: Her bangs hang low on her forehead, and she wears a little bun on top of her head.

28

YES! flat on top   NO! not round

3

4

bangs are a
little poufy

mouth
is low
on face

Tinker Bell
has a very
upturned nose

5

Tinker Bell

Because we can't understand what Tinker Bell is saying when she is with Peter and the others, the expressions on her face and her body language are important: They tell you when she is happy, angry, and even jealous. Her tiny costume adds to her pixie look and helps her fly about freely. But don't forget to draw her wings—she couldn't fly without them!

Tinker Bell is about 4-1/2 heads tall

1

2

body is heavier on bottom than on top

YES! legs curve out at thighs and calves

NO! legs don't taper from thick to thin

3

5

4

...rt is short
...d flares a bit
...ottom

YES! ragged bottom edge

NO! not even shapes

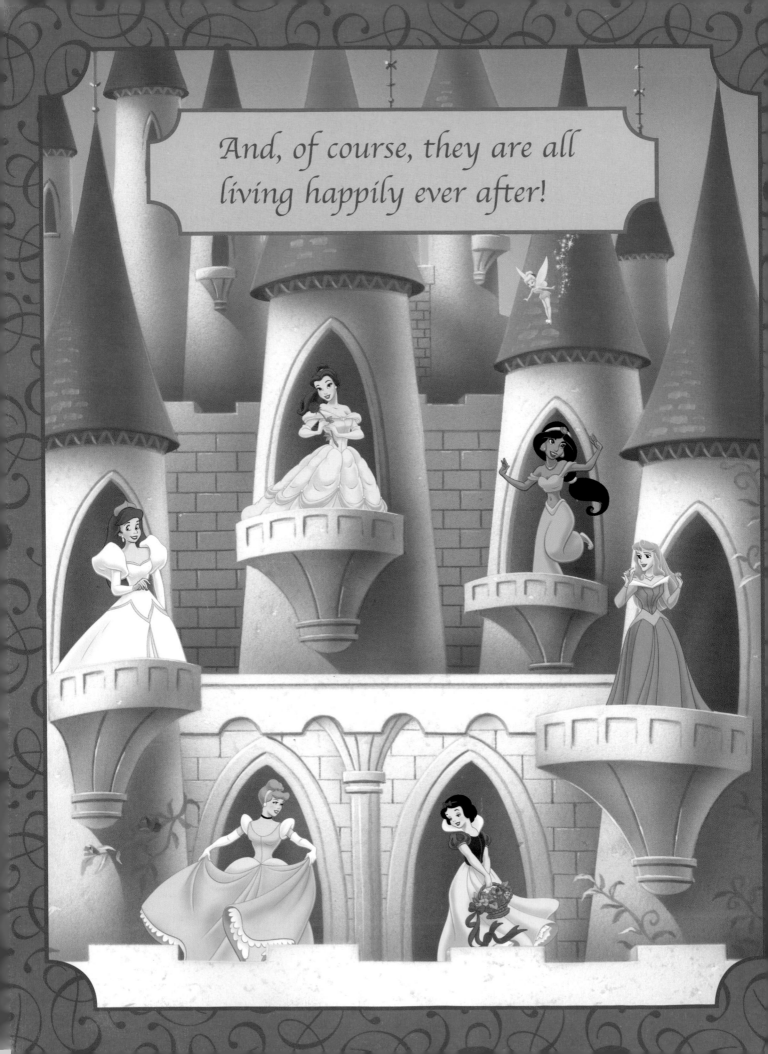

And, of course, they are all living happily ever after!